Beyond the Cage

Escaping Learned Helplessness

Freudian Trips

Copyright Page

© 2023 by Freudian Trips

All rights reserved. No part of this book may be reproduced in any form or by any electronic or mechanical means, including information storage and retrieval systems, without permission in writing from the publisher, except by a reviewer who may quote brief passages in a review.

This book is a work of non-fiction. Unless otherwise noted, the author and the publisher make no explicit guarantees as to the accuracy of the information contained in this book and will not be held responsible for any errors or omissions.

Published by Omniterra Media Inc

First Edition

Visit the author's website at www.freudiantrips.com

Disclaimer

The views and opinions expressed in this book are those of the author(s) and do not necessarily reflect the official policy or position of any other agency, organization, employer, or company. The contents of this book are for informational and educational purposes only and are not intended to serve as professional advice, diagnosis, or treatment.

The information provided in this book is believed to be accurate and reliable as of the date of publication. However, it may include some errors or inaccuracies, and no warranty or guarantee is provided regarding the accuracy, timeliness, or applicability of the content.

Readers are encouraged to consult with professional philosophers, educators, or other qualified professionals where appropriate for personalized advice. The author(s) and publisher shall not be liable for any loss, damage, or harm caused or alleged to be caused, directly or indirectly, by the information or ideas contained, suggested, or referenced in this book.

By reading this book, the reader acknowledges and agrees that they are solely responsible for how they interpret and apply the information contained herein.

This book may also include references to other works, studies, and sources. These references are provided for further reading and exploration and do not imply endorsement or validation of the specific theories, viewpoints, or interpretations presented in those works.

Introduction: The Trap of Helplessness

Imagine feeling like nothing you do matters. You try and try, but things never seem to change. After a while, you might just give up. That feeling of being trapped, unable to control your situation, is at the core of something called "learned helplessness."

At first glance, the name seems strange. After all, shouldn't helplessness be something we're born with? In this case, it's actually something we learn. It happens when we experience repeated situations where it seems like our actions don't have any effect – no matter what we do, things stay the same or get worse. Slowly, we begin to believe that we have no power to make things better.

The Heavy Toll

Learned helplessness isn't just a bad feeling; it can have serious consequences. Think of someone stuck in a miserable job for years, believing they'll never find anything else. Or a student who always gets bad grades, so they simply stop trying. It can lead to:

Depression: That deep-down sadness and loss of hope.

Anxiety: Constant worry and fear because nothing feels safe or predictable.

Giving Up: Not even trying to improve things, losing motivation completely.

Why is This So Common Today?

Unfortunately, modern life can be a breeding ground for learned helplessness. Think about it:

Endless Bad News: We're always bombarded with reports of problems, disasters, things beyond our control.

Lack of Community: Many people feel isolated, like they have no one to turn to for help or support.

"Comparison Culture": Social media makes us feel like everyone else is doing better, making our problems feel unfixable.

The Good News

The most important thing about learned helplessness is that it doesn't have to be permanent. It's called "learned" for a reason – and just like we can learn to feel helpless, we can also learn how to break free and feel empowered again.

Chapter 1: Where It All Began – Understanding the Science

Think back to science class in school. To really understand something, you often did experiments, right? Well, the idea of learned helplessness started the same way. It all began with a scientist named Martin Seligman and some experiments with dogs.

The Experiment That Changed Everything

Seligman and his team divided dogs into three groups. Here's what happened:

Group 1: Briefly got a mild electric shock but had a way to stop it by pressing a lever.

Group 2: Got the same shock as Group 1, but no matter what they did, they couldn't stop it.

Group 3: No shocks –they just relaxed.

Later, the dogs were put in a different situation – a box they could easily escape from to avoid the shocks. Can you guess what happened?

Group 1 & 3: Learned to escape the box quickly.

Group 2: Many didn't even try to escape. They'd learned the shocks were unavoidable, so they simply endured them.

Uncontrollability: The Key Ingredient

The big takeaway was this: it's not just bad experiences that mess us up, it's feeling like we have no control over them. When we believe nothing we do matters, we tend to become passive, even when there's actually a way out.

What Happens in Our Brains

Now, this isn't just about how we feel; there's science happening in our brains too! When we're in uncontrollable situations, certain pathways in our brains get super active, while areas involved in taking action and problem-solving get quieter. It's like our brains also learn to be helpless.

Important Note: This doesn't mean people who experience difficult situations are weak! Our brains are amazingly adaptable, but sometimes they learn patterns that aren't helpful long-term. The good news is, we can retrain our brains just like we retrain our muscles!

Chapter 2: Stuck in the Cycle – How Helplessness Takes Hold

Imagine you have a really difficult puzzle. You try for ages, but you just can't figure it out, and you eventually toss it aside in frustration. A few days later, you see the puzzle again and think, "Ugh, forget it. I'm terrible at puzzles." You don't even try.

That's similar to how learned helplessness becomes a habit. The more times we feel stuck in situations we can't control, the stronger that feeling of helplessness gets.

The Vicious Cycle

Here's how the cycle of learned helplessness works:

Uncontrollable Experience: Something bad happens, and we feel powerless to change it (a job loss, a failing grade, a breakup, etc.).

Expectation of Failure: We start to believe that even if a different situation comes along, things still won't work out.

Inaction: We stop trying. Why bother if we're bound to fail anyway?

Negative Outcome: Because we don't try, we don't succeed. This reinforces our belief that we can't control anything.

Back to the Beginning: The cycle starts all over again.

Helplessness's Sidekicks: Depression and Anxiety

This cycle can be a major contributor to depression and anxiety:

Depression: It makes us feel sad, hopeless, and lose motivation to even try basic things.

Anxiety: We worry constantly because the world feels unsafe; if we have no control, bad things could happen at any time.

It's like our brains are stuck on a broken record, playing the same sad, scary song over and over.

The Key Is Breaking the Cycle

Learning about this cycle is the first step toward breaking it. Just realizing that our thoughts and past experiences influence our current actions is a powerful thing. The next chapters will be all about how to change this pattern and find our way back to feeling in control!

Chapter 3: Not All Helplessness Is Created Equal

Think of learned helplessness like a bad case of the flu: there are different strains, and some hit harder than others. It's helpful to understand these different "strains" so we can figure out the best way to tackle them.

Two Big Questions

We can sort learned helplessness into types by asking two key questions:

How Widespread Is It?

Specific: Feeling helpless about one area of life (like bad at math, unlucky in love)

Global: Feeling helpless about almost everything, like a dark cloud over your whole life.

How Long Does It Last?

Unstable: Feeling helpless due to a temporary situation (bad week at work, a single failed test).

Stable: Feeling like you'll always be helpless, no matter what.

Blame Game: Internal vs. External

There's one more way we categorize helplessness: how we explain it to ourselves.

Internal: "It's my fault." Believing bad things happen because you're not good enough, smart enough, etc.

External: "The world is unfair." Believing it's always bad luck, other people, the system rigged against you.

Why Does This Matter?

Understanding the type of learned helplessness helps in two ways:

Pinpointing the Problem: Is it one specific area, or does it feel like your whole world is out of control? Does it come and go, or is it always with you?

Finding the Right Solution: Specific helplessness is easier to fix with direct action (math tutoring, social skills practice). Global and stable types, especially with internal blame, often need help working on our thoughts and beliefs alongside taking action.

Important Note: Even "smaller" cases of learned helplessness deserve attention. They can grow more serious if left unchecked!

Chapter 4: Helplessness Hiding in Plain Sight

Learned helplessness isn't just something that happens in a science lab. It can creep into all sorts of everyday situations. Let's take a look:

Relationships: The Trap of Staying Stuck

A person in an unhappy relationship who believes they'll never find anyone better, so they don't try to leave.

Someone who feels like they always mess up friendships, so they stop reaching out and become isolated.

A child trapped in a household with conflict, feeling they can't do anything to make things better.

Work & Career: When Dreams Fade

The employee overlooked for promotions so often they stop putting in extra effort.

Someone who wants to change careers but thinks it's "too late" and they'll never succeed in something new.

The constant fear of layoffs making workers feel powerless, even if they're doing great work.

Education: Giving Up on Learning

The student constantly getting bad grades, making them believe they're "just not smart" and stop studying.

Children from disadvantaged backgrounds feeling like the system is against them, so they don't see the point in trying.

Adults who wish they could go back to school, but believe they'd fail, so they don't even explore options.

Feeling Small in a Big World: Social Issues

People overwhelmed by news of wars, disasters, etc., thinking their individual actions don't make a difference.

Feeling like voting is pointless because politicians are "all the same" and nothing will change.

Communities plagued by problems like poverty or crime where people feel trapped in their circumstances.

Important to Remember

These are just examples, and it's not about blaming the individual! Many of these situations involve real, unfair obstacles. The point is: when repeated setbacks and a sense of no control combine, even strong people can start to feel helpless.

Why Does This Matter?

Seeing learned helplessness "in the wild" helps us understand two things:

You're Not Alone: If you recognize yourself in these examples, you're far from the only one struggling with these feelings.

It Has Consequences: Learned helplessness doesn't just hurt us personally, it can hold back whole communities and keep society from improving.

Chapter 5: The Escape Plan – Finding Your Way Back to Control

Remember those dogs in the experiment who just sat and endured the shocks? The good news is, we're not dogs! Humans have amazing brains, capable of change and learning new things. Breaking free from learned helplessness is a journey, but there are proven ways to do it.

Toolkit Time: Strategies for Fighting Back

We'll tackle this in two main ways: changing your thoughts and taking action.

Mental Makeover: Cognitive Techniques

Reality Check Your Inner Critic: Our brains love to tell us stories like "I'll never..." or "I'm always unlucky." Learn to spot these exaggerated thoughts and challenge them with evidence!

Dispute the Doom: Ask questions like, "Is this really true?" or "What would I tell a friend who thought this way?"

Focus on What You CAN Control: There's likely something you can influence, even if it's small. Zeroing in on that helps build your power back up.

Action Steps: Behavioral Techniques

Baby Steps Win the Race: Start ridiculously small with goals that feel easy to achieve. A tiny success is still a success!

Embrace the Experiment: Try new things, even with fear of failure. The point is to prove that outcomes aren't always set in stone.

Celebrate Your Mastery: Whenever you succeed, even in small ways, remind yourself you did that! Builds proof that your actions matter.

The Power of People: Support Systems

Therapists: Your Brain Trainers: They specialize in techniques (like Cognitive Behavioral Therapy) perfect for fighting learned helplessness.

Finding Your Cheer Squad: Supportive friends, family, or groups fighting similar battles make a huge difference.

Inspiration Matters: Hearing success stories of people who overcame obstacles builds your belief in what's possible.

Key Points to Remember

Be Patient: Changing lifelong thought patterns takes time – like training for a marathon, not a sprint.

Slip-Ups are Normal: Nobody's perfect. If you fall back into old thinking, be kind to yourself and get back on track.

Your Control Muscle Grows Stronger: The more you practice these techniques, the easier they get, and the more empowered you'll feel!

Chapter 6: From Surviving to Thriving – Building Your Resilience Arsenal

Overcoming learned helplessness is a fantastic start, but the real goal is to avoid falling back into that trap. This is where resilience comes in – it's like your mental immune system against helplessness!

Upgrading Your Coping Skills

Problem-Solving Mode: Instead of giving up when things are tough, practice a step-by-step approach: What's the problem? What are some possible solutions? What can I do right now, even if it's small?

Prepare, Don't Panic: Brainstorm ahead about potential challenges and ways you might handle them. This gives you control even when life throws curveballs.

Healthy Outlets: Find ways to manage stress and emotions that work for you – exercise, creative hobbies, relaxation techniques – they're essential tools.

Mindfulness: Your Secret Weapon

The Noticing Game: Pay attention to your thoughts and feelings without judgment. Spot those early signs of helplessness creeping in, so you can address them!

Breathe Through It: Simple techniques like deep breathing calm your nervous system and clear your head when overwhelmed.

Self-Compassion is Key: Be kind to yourself as you work on this - everyone struggles sometimes.

Goals: Your Road Map to Empowerment

Small & Achievable: Tiny goals you know you can accomplish build confidence over time.

Meaningful to YOU: Don't pick goals just because someone else thinks you should - focus on what matters to you.

Celebrate Every Milestone: Recognizing your progress makes reaching bigger goals feel more possible.

Motivation That Lasts: Fueling Yourself

Intrinsic Motivation: This means doing things because they give you joy, satisfaction, or align with your values. It's far more powerful than rewards or pressure.

Rediscover Your "Why": What gets you excited? What kind of person do you want to be? Connect your actions to this bigger picture.

Surround Yourself with the Right Fuel: People who believe in you, environments that foster growth – these are essential for long-lasting motivation.

Remember: Resilience isn't about never struggling, it's about knowing you can cope with challenges, learn from them, and keep moving forward.

Chapter 7: Own Your Story – The Power of Agency

Think of the word "agency". It's about having a say in your life, not just being swept along by whatever happens. That's the ultimate destination after escaping learned helplessness. Here's how to get there:

Mindset Makeover: Optimism & Growth

Optimism (The Realistic Kind): This doesn't mean believing everything will be perfect. It's about trusting you can handle challenges and finding the good even in tough times.

Growth Mindset: Believing that your abilities aren't fixed – you can learn, improve, and overcome setbacks with effort. This makes challenges feel less defeating.

Your Why: The Compass for Your Journey

What Drives You?: What values are most important? What gives your life meaning? (Helping others, creativity, building a better community – it's deeply personal!)

Decisions Big and Small: Connecting your choices to this bigger purpose helps you stay on course, even when things are hard.

Flexible, Not Rigid: Our purpose can evolve over time, that's normal! Check in regularly to make sure your path still aligns with your values.

Staying Strong: Preventing Relapse

Triggers & Warning Signs: Know what situations or thoughts tend to set off that old helpless feeling. Then, you can have a plan ready!

Reflection is Your Friend: Check in with yourself regularly: How am I feeling? What am I thinking? This helps catch slipping into negative patterns early.

Maintenance Mode: The tools you learned are for life! Regular use keeps your "resilience muscles" strong.

The Gift of Choice

Maybe you didn't choose the experiences that made you feel helpless. But from here on out, you have more choices than you think. You can choose how you respond to challenges, what mindset you cultivate, and what kind of life you want to build.

Imagine this...

A few years from now, you run into a tough situation (it happens to everyone!). Instead of feeling crushed, you think, "This sucks, but I've dealt with hard stuff before. Let's figure this out." That's the true power of overcoming learned helplessness!

Conclusion: The Choice is Yours

Throughout this book, we've explored a simple, yet profound idea: learned helplessness is exactly that – something learned. And if it's learned, it can be unlearned. Let's recap some of the most important things to remember:

You Are Not Alone: Countless people struggle with feelings of helplessness – it's part of being human in a complex world.

Change is Possible: Your brain is amazing! With the right tools and practice, you can rewire those old patterns of thinking and action.

Small Steps, Big Impact: Even the tiniest acts of taking charge can start to build a sense of control and confidence.

Resilience is a Skill: The more you practice overcoming challenges, the stronger and more capable you become.

Your Purpose is Your North Star: Connecting with what truly matters to you fuels your motivation and guides your direction.

The Transformation

Overcoming learned helplessness isn't just about feeling better; it changes how you experience life. Imagine:

Approaching problems with curiosity instead of dread.

Seeing setbacks as opportunities to learn, not confirmation you're "not good enough."

Trusting yourself to make choices that shape the life you want.

A Call to Action

This book isn't the end of the journey, it's the beginning. Here's what you can do right now:

Reflect: Where do you notice learned helplessness showing up in your life? Pick one area to start with.

Choose One Tool: Pick a technique from the book you want to try this week. Keep it simple to start!

Seek Support: It could be a therapist, a trusted friend, an online group – sharing the journey makes it easier.

The Power in Your Hands

The world will always have challenges. Learned helplessness convinces us that we're powerless against them. But that's simply not true. You have the ability to choose how you think, act, and respond. Embrace that power. Reclaim your sense of control, bit by bit. The life you build from there is yours to create.

About Freudian Trips

Welcome to Freudian Trips, your dedicated platform for diving deep into the world of psychology. We are more than just a YouTube channel or a book publisher. We are a beacon of enlightenment, making complex psychological concepts accessible and engaging for all.

Our YouTube channel is a rich repository of psychology made simple. We take the profound and often complex ideas from the world of psychology and break them down into digestible, easy-to-understand content. From the foundational theories of Freud to the cognitive insights of Piaget, we cover a broad spectrum of psychological schools and thoughts, making psychology accessible to everyone, regardless of their background or prior knowledge.

As a book publisher, we take the same approach, transforming intricate psychological theories into comprehensible narratives. Our books are not just collections of words, but vessels of wisdom that make psychology approachable and relatable. We believe that psychology should not be confined to academic circles, but should be available to all who seek to understand the human mind and behavior.

At Freudian Trips, we believe in the power of curiosity and the pursuit of knowledge. We are here to stoke the fires of your curiosity, to guide you on your intellectual journey, and to help you navigate the fascinating world of psychology.

If you are someone who is not afraid to question, to explore, and to learn, then you are in the right place. Join us on this journey of exploration, as we make psychology easy to understand, one concept at a time.

Be sure to visit our Youtube channel at: www.freudiantrips.com/youtube

You can also visit us on the web at www.freudiantrips.com

Welcome to The Freudian Trip community. Stay curious. Stay enlightened.

Printed in Great Britain
by Amazon